2024 Ellen Nancy, Roxanne Reid & Anastasia Dragunova
I'm not afraid
Printed by Ingramspark.
HB Publishing House, 21, NG13 7AW
British Library Catalogue in Publication Data: a catalogue record for this book is available from the British Library.
ISBN 9781068642708

I'm not afraid

Ellen Nancy & Roxanne Reid

Illustrated by Anastasia Dragunova

Herbie the hedgehog was a long way from home. He knew the only way to his cosy den was through the deep, dark forest, so he set off on his journey.

The cold wind whistled through the forest and sent shivers to the very ends of Herbie's spines.

"I am not afraid of the whistling wind," he said.
Herbie kept on going. He was determined to get home.

Leaves rustled under his paws.
The sticky, wet mud made his
claws curl.

"I am not afraid of the wet,
sticky mud," he said.
Herbie kept on going.

He stomped his way through the
muddy leaves, keeping his eyes on
the track through the trees.

Ahead, Herbie saw
the old bridge.

He stepped out and the bridge
creaked and groaned. He could see
the wild river, rushing underneath
him.
"I am not afraid of the wild river," he
said. Herbie kept on going.
He shuffled his way carefully across
the rickety bridge - only daring to
glance down at the very end.

On the other side of the river, Herbie heard a rustling in the long grass. He stood still. What creature was hiding, ready to pounce?

"I am not afraid of the rustling grass," he said.

Herbie kept on going.
He quietly tiptoed through the
grass, checking left and right for
the pointed ears of a fox.

The sun began to set. The sky turned red. The trees cast long, spooky shadows that made him jump.

"I am not afraid of the spooky shadows," he said. Herbie kept on going.

He lifted his chin and did not look at the shadows on the ground.

The sun set behind the trees and Herbie felt eyes watching him from above. Wings flapped. Shining eyes glowed in the dark.

"I am not afraid of watching eyes," he said. Herbie kept on going. He moved from tree to tree in the direction of his den.

As Herbie inched closer to home,
the forest came alive with the
sounds of the night. Owls hooted
overhead; badgers snuffled in the
dirt. Herbie began to walk a little
faster.

"I am not afraid of the noise," he
said. Herbie kept on going.
He hummed a little tune to take his
mind off the sounds around him.

The darkness swallowed up the forest. Herbie couldn't see past the end of his nose.

Finally, he saw the familiar glimmer of the light over the door of his den.

"I am not afraid of the dark," he said.
Herbie kept on going.
His pace quickened. He raced to his front door.

Safe and sound in his cosy home, Herbie looked up at the night sky. The stars twinkled brightly and the moon shone. Herbie smiled. He had made it home, despite maybe being a little afraid. But he told himself, "I am not afraid of anything."

Herbie made a cup of hot milk
and settled in for a warm
night's sleep, feeling rather
brave.

If you like this book, check out these titles by Ellen Nancy and Roxanne Reid.

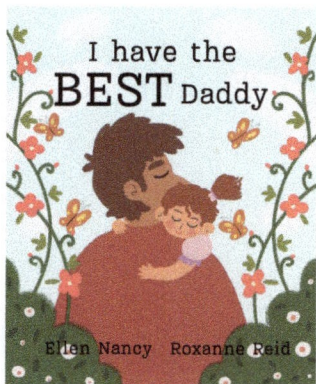

The perfect book for Father's Day or Daddy's birthday.

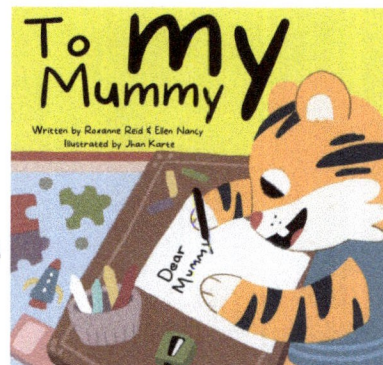

The perfect book for Mother's Day or Mummy's birthday.

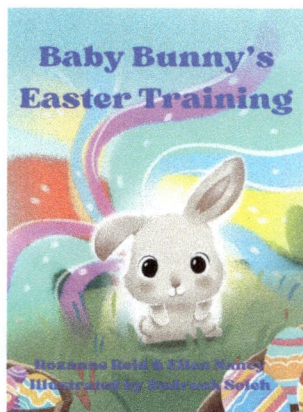

The perfect book to share at Easter.

BOOK REVIEW

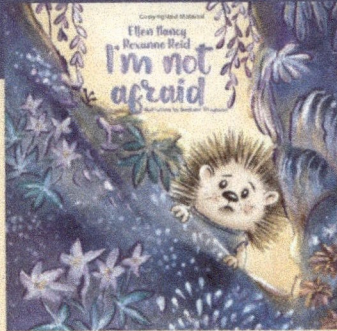

This is one of the most inspiring books I've read in a long time!

The adorable character of Herbie couldn't be more perfect for teaching readers bravery and determination. The mantra he repeats to himself is what makes this book so powerful.

Louise Jane, CEO
The Golden Wizard Book Prize

Let's be friends...

www.hbpublishinghouse.co.uk

hb_publishing_house

HB Publishing House

hb_publishing_house

HB
PUBLISHING HOUSE

Draw Herbie on his journey

www.ingramcontent.com/pod-product-compliance
Lightning Source LLC
Chambersburg PA
CBHW040253100426
42811CB00011B/1244

9 781068 642708